Investing

How To Read And Analyze Balance Sheets For Effective Implementation: A Step-by-step Guide

(The Psychology Of Investing And Behavioral Finance Explained)

Terrance Martinez

TABLE OF CONTENT

Market Trends 1
Why The Materialist Point Of View Is False 20
Behavioural Control 34
Is Investing In Non-Fungible Tokens Worthwhile?
.... 47
Where Can I Invest In Assets? 58
Property Investment's Benefits And Drawbacks 67
Various Forms Of Financial Investment 78
Learning The Investment Rules 88
Using Etfs To Combine Passive And Active Investing
.... 106
Investments 119
Index Funds 138

Market Trends

To Leverage Your Everyday Investments, You Must Be Knowledgeable About The Options Market. Simply Because There Are Many Similarities Between The Subtleties Of Options And Stocks, Many Day Traders Start Out On The Stock Market. In Fact, When Most People Hear The Term "Day Trading," They Instantly Think Of Trading Stocks. Therefore, Even Though Traders Should Never Conflate The Two, It Is In Everyone's Best Interest To Learn About The Stock Market. The Purpose Of This Chapter Is To Enlighten You About The Market Factors That Might Effect Your Success.

Selecting A Market For Trading

You Must Determine What Asset Classes Are Suitable For Day Trading Options Before Entering The Market To Hunt For Options To Trade. If You Don't, The Market Might Appear Limitless And Will

Just Leave You Feeling Confused And Befuddled. Stocks Are The Straightforward, Well-Liked Option, But They Are Not The Only One, And They May Not Be The Best One For You. Day Trading Choices Include Futures, Foreign Exchange, Cryptocurrencies, And Even Corn. The Purchase And Sale Of Shares From A Company's Portfolio Facilitates Stock Trading, And On The American Stock Market, Day Trading Stock Options Necessitates That All Positions Be Started By 9:30 Am Est And Closed By 4 Pm Est. In The Futures Market, A Contract Is Established Between The Seller And The Trader To Purchase Or Sell An Associated Asset At A Fixed Price At A Later Time. The Price Changes That Might Occur Within A Day Can Be Profitable For An Options Day Trader. The Operating Hours Of The Futures Market Might Fluctuate, Therefore The Day Trader Has To Exercise Caution. As A Result, The Trader Must Be Aware Of The Deadline For Closing A Position. The Largest Financial Market In The World And One

That Is Open 24/7 Is The Currency Market. Different Currencies May Be Exchanged On This Market. When Beginning Your Options Day Trading Career, There Are Many More Markets To Choose From, But Ultimately It Comes Down To Your Situation And The Resources You Have At Your Disposal. The Startup Money, For Instance, Can Be A Problem. The Stock Market Is Where This Is Most Common. In Order To Trade On The Stock Market, A Trader Must Have More Than $20,000 In Their Trading Account, But The Forex Market Permits Transactions As Little As A Few Hundred Dollars. So, Unless You Have The Necessary Funding, You Cannot Explore Options In The Stock And Futures Markets.

Time Is Still Another Factor. Keep In Mind That Certain Markets, Such As The Stock Market, Only Operate During Specific Hours, While Others Are Open 24 Hours A Day.

Another Element Is The Approach. Some Techniques Are More Effective In A

Particular Market At Particular Times Of The Day, And We Shall Discuss This In A Later Chapter. Therefore, If A Day Trader Excels At A Certain Approach, They May See Superior Success In Particular Markets.

The Best Options To Day Trade: How To Find Them

You May Choose Which Specific Assets You Will Chase Options In Once You Have Decided On A Market In Which To Invest. Fortunately, There Are Mechanisms In Place That May Assist You In Identifying Profitable Niches. These Tools Consist Of:

Technical Assessment

This Is The First Tool We'll Talk About. Day Traders May Use It To Analyze Market Segments To Find Strengths And Weaknesses. The Options Day Trader Might Focus On The Options Niches They Would Want To Explore Inside A Certain Market By Determining Those Strengths And Shortcomings.

To Undertake Technical Analysis, A Variety Of Instruments Are Available, Including:

Bollinger Band, A Gauge Of Market Turbulence.

Intraday Momentum Index (Imi), A Predictor Of How Options Will Behave Over The Course Of A Single Day.

Options Trends Are Determined Using Open Interest (Oi), Which Represents The Quantity Of Open Options.

Money Flow Index (Mfi), Which Depicts How Much Money Has Been Invested In Various Types Of Assets Over A Certain Period Of Time.

Relative Strength Index (Rsi), Which Enables The Trader To Contrast Gains And Losses Over A Predetermined Time Frame.

Put-Call Ratio (Pcr), Which Shows How Often Put Options Are Traded In Comparison To Call Options.

Price Diagrams

In Order To Identify Market Patterns, These Tools Provide A Visual Depiction Of Price And Volume Information. Charts Occur In Many Forms And Are More Specifically Known As Price Charts Since They Display Price Movement Over A Certain Period Of Time. Typical Kinds Are:

Line Diagrams

These Simple-To-Understand Charts Show How Prices Have Changed Over A Certain Time Frame, Such Months Or Years. A Single Line Connects Each Pricing Data Point. While Simplicity Is The Primary Benefit Of This Style Of Chart, Day Traders Are At A Disadvantage Since It Gives No Indication Of How Strong Trading Is Throughout The Day. Additionally, The Line Chart Does Not Include Data On The Price Gap. The Distance Between One Trading Session That Is Entirely Above Or Below A Prior Trading Period Is Known As A Price Gap. For Options Day Traders To Make Wise Selections, They

Need Access To This Price Cap Information.

Closed-High-Low-Open Bar Diagram

This kind of chart shows the change of prices over certain time periods, such an hour or a day, from highest to lowest. Its name derives from the fact that it displays the open, high, low, and close prices for the given time frame. The opening and closing prices are shown on a horizontal tab, and the low to high trading range is shown with a vertical line. The chart shows movement over a long period of time as a succession of bars, each of which has all four aspects.

Due to the information it gives on 1-day trading periods as well as price gap knowledge, this style of bar chart is helpful as a tool for options day trading.

Chart using candles

Professional options day traders use a chart similar to this one. Price is shown on the vertical axis and time is shown on the horizontal axis, like an open-high-low-close bar chart. As a result, it shows how prices change over time.

Individual elements make up the candlestick chart's structure. They are known as candlesticks, which is how the chart got its name. Three pieces make up each candlestick. They are known as:

The Body: This represents the spectrum from wide to narrow.

The Wick: This symbolizes the highs and lows of the day. The shadow is another name for it.

The color: This shows how prices are moving in that way. An rising price movement is indicated by white or green. A fall in price is indicated by red or black.

Day traders may identify market trends by using the candlestick chart. There are several candlestick chart types.

Various Elements That Impact the Options Market

It's time to explore the market and place a wager on the options you've chosen after analyzing the options market and deciding which ones you'll pursue.

To begin with, you must complete a transaction. You will place an order via the broker's electronic system if you are utilizing an online broker, which is how most options day traders operate these days. The options day trader must decide whether or not to initiate a new position or close an existing one after doing this.

The transaction information will be electronically provided to the options day trader when this has been successfully done.

Interest rates, societal trends, and market volatility are all variables that will impact how the option will perform.

Chapter Overview

To be successful in this line of work, an options day trader must be familiar with the options market. The day trader's initial task is to choose the specific market in which he or she would trade options. The stock market is a well-liked alternative, but it has established hours for options trading and demands a large initial commitment.

Popular options trading venues with varying working hours and lower minimum initial investment requirements include the futures and forex markets. Some day traders who trade options may find these more effective.

The options day trader must choose a specific niche within that market to trade options in after determining the specific market in which he or she will trade options. Options day traders choose the best options to pursue by using technical analysis and price charts including the line chart, open-high-low-close bar chart, and candlestick chart.

The day trader will use the brokerage company they deal with to carry out the options transaction after making this choice. Since most options day traders use digital methods in this day and age of technology, this is often done online. Interest rates, economic trends, and market volatility are some of the variables that will determine how well this options strategy performs.

Why does this approach work so well for part-time wholesalers?

All real estate investors have one thing in common: at some time, you either didn't own any property or you had made an offer to acquire one. Everyone has to start somewhere, and it's unusual for someone to begin investing in real estate without doing so first part-time while holding down another career. Working in corporate America during your free time while pursuing bigger and better opportunities may be that job.

The conventional 40-hour work week is a myth, particularly when you include in travel time to and from work as well as any additional hours necessary to maintain good working relations with your employer.

So, yes, maintaining your real estate marketing strategy while juggling business obligations can take time. At first, you may think everything is fine and lovely, but scheduling meetings with merchants when it's convenient for them might be really challenging.

Making the most of your time is important whether or not you have a regular job, so being innovative in certain ways is essential. A strong, consistent marketing strategy may really aid your business in this situation.

When you first start out, it's simple to waste time looking for vendors that are motivated. It's much better if motivated vendors get in touch with you. Here is a technique that will make you happy that you have a mailbox, whether or not you are short on time.

Once merchants start calling you, you may pre-screen them on the phone to gauge their degree of motivation. launch by the property to see if it is vacant or abandoned (you may then launch postal campaigns that are specific to those kinds of properties). Based on information from public sources, what the seller told you, and your own experience evaluating neighborhoods and homes, calculate your statistics.

Then, without even negotiating with the seller, submit an all-cash offer for the house and send the latter a contract.

That seems a little weird, doesn't it? However, it does save a ton of time, particularly if you're pressed for time.

Include two signed copies of the contract along with a lovely cover letter detailing your contract offer. Mark the areas where they should sign and date with post-it notes, and instruct them to ship back one copy to you in the self-addressed, stamped envelope while retaining the other copy for their records.

You no longer need several sneaky clauses in your contract. The agreement must be made conditional upon, among other things, establishing unambiguous title and access to the property. You need access to the property so that you may do more inspections and exhibit it to your prospective rehab buyer(s). If you're going to play the game in this manner, you'll need to be able to accurately estimate a property's current condition as well as the necessary repairs. You'll need to be particularly adept at figuring out what type of repairs are necessary to properly analyze the deal if you are unable to enter the house to view it.

The little package, which includes postage, a return envelope, and a letter, comes together for around $1.50. You'll be surprised (really astonished) when those contracts that you signed are returned to you in the mail. If you have a significant number of out-of-town sellers, this service is great. This is a choice that makes the most of your time while keeping you in the game if you can't meet with merchants on their schedule, even if they live in your city.

After sending the contract offer, keep a copy on hand, and make a note in your tickler or to-do list file to get in touch with the seller if you haven't heard back by a certain date. You will commonly be informed, "You should have it back in the mail to you by now," when you call the vendor to find out whether they received your shipment.

Of fact, more often than not, the offer will be far less than what people anticipate, and that is precisely how you should present the offer. Call it lowball offers or whatever you like, but you want to get a good deal on a property. Even if the seller calls you back or you get in touch with them again and they let you know the offer wasn't accepted, that's great! You're at least trying to negotiate, and you now have a benchmark that offers them a price range you can live with.

They may now engage in play and provide counterproposals. If the counteroffer is too far off the mark, just smile and keep the door open—you never know what could transpire later. Many things might change as time goes on.

Depending on how you perceive the seller's motive, there could be a chance there. One wholesaler, for instance, sent a vendor a $9,000 postal offer as a starting point. She had the idea that it may cost about $40,000!

They certainly didn't fit in there very well. After much haggling, they settled on $12,000 as their compromise. Don't let an early, unreasonably low counteroffer discourage you if you can see the seller is motivated.

It could seem odd to do business by mail with a seller you have never seen or spoken to in person. The rehab buyer will close and finance that morning with the attorney, and the seller will arrive later that afternoon to complete a conventional simultaneous closing. You will talk on the phone often to ensure that everything is going well throughout the closing. The lawyer or title company will mail you your check if you are unable to attend the closing or drive down to pick it up. Therefore, even if you just visit a house once, you can still be able to gain money by simply making a few more phone calls. Although it is ideal to meet the seller in person, don't be discouraged if you are unable to do so with every motivated seller you come across.But if you don't have enough time to meet with every motivated seller you talk with, that's okay. If you're creative, you can still earn a lot of money by wholesaling properties!

You're well on your way to making money rapidly now that you know the key to finding motivated sellers of houses that you can wholesale. With a comprehensive marketing effort that includes bandit signs, fliers, driving for money, and other promotional materials, you will be able to wholesale a lot more deals. However, the simplest way to profit from home wholesaling is to focus data on absentee owners. As you begin visiting wholesale houses, maybe you'll be eager to put everything you've learned about direct mail to use.

Why The Materialist Point Of View Is False

The falsity of Scientific Materialism, the tenet upon which science is taught in schools, must be publicly acknowledged and embraced as the new zeitgeist. The incorrect premise, according to the Foreword, is that there is such a thing as material substance, or "matter".

Intelligent life and awareness would not have been conceivable before the development of the brain, if matter were the only thing that existed. And if that's the case, a mind is necessary for awareness to exist. If this is the case, then we may compare humans to computers since they have brains that are similar to computers. These are intricate component assemblies that will ultimately wear out and decompose.

When the body dies, the lights will go out, and that will be the last of us.

If this is the case, why even bother trying to achieve self-actualization? Why attempt to make it a wonderful life if a virus or other sickness may take it away? You can give into nihilism right now and throw everything away. If committing suicide doesn't appeal to you, how about using painkillers to prolong your high or living in a crack house and relying on government assistance?

Reality cannot be seen from a materialist perspective. After Darwin published The Origin of Species (1859), this perspective on reality became more widely accepted. Science was still in its infancy at the time, and it had a lot to learn before it could go beyond this stage. Back then, scientists were not aware that microorganisms might cause illness. Bacteria was seen as a symptom rather than a cause. Instead of the packets of vibrating energy known as electrons or quarks, the atoms that make up matter were considered to resemble small marbles. Life's origin in a primordial lagoon with the correct ingredients was thought to be an accident. Unexpectedly, and this is the issue, scientists still hold that belief. It seems that individuals who are aware of the truth are either terrified of being mocked or worry that it would spark a religious resurgence.

There was a lot of work done that increased our understanding between 1859 and 1957. But let's go forward to that period. The double helix DNA's chemical components may be thought of as digital characters, such as the ones and zeros in computer code, or as alphabetic letters in written languages, according to Francis Crick (1916–1964).

DNA code prints have undoubtedly been observed before. Crick revealed that they are in charge of assembling the machinery and proteins required for cells to live. It was evident that the development of essential elements in living cells was facilitated by digital information. We need to explain how this intricate processing system came to be in order to understand the beginnings of life.

It's not that difficult. According to the website of BBC Science Focus Magazine, the nucleus of an organism has 46 chromosomes worth of DNA. Natural helical molecules like DNA are super-coiled by enzymes to occupy less space. The length of DNA in a single cell would be around two meters. The total amount of DNA in your cells would therefore be around double the size of the Solar System.

This is incredible! The length of one DNA strand is six feet. Given the modest size of the codes, this must contain a lot of code. There is a lot of information in there. How could a lightning strike in a primordial lake's chemical mix produce a microscopic strand of six-foot-long computer-like codes? Can't be done.

The URL to the article I just referenced is as follows: https://www.sciencefocus.com/the-human-body/how-long-is-yourdna/

It is evident that there is an intellectual input behind every piece of information we encounter and can track back to its original source, whether it be code, a passage from a book, or a computer program. This demonstrates that all life originates from intellect. Dedicated Scientific Materialists, however, believe that everything is possible through accident. For instance, War and Peace and all of Shakespeare's works may be ultimately produced by a room full of monkeys with typewriters. Just a question of time, then. It is difficult to picture mathematicians estimating the odds of it really occurring, if not impossible.

The truth is that DNA was not produced randomly. The Big Bang, according to scientists, is thought to have occurred about 13.8 billion years ago, creating the universe. At this time, the world is 4.5 billion years old. Scientists estimate that life first appeared on Earth 3.77 billion years ago. There is still a 730 million year window in which someone may have created tiny code measuring six feet, six inches long. The probabilities that it might occur have been estimated by mathematicians. True, some scientists reject the notion that the cosmos was created. They think that the cosmos has always been and that it is constantly expanding and contracting. Whether it has a beginning, has always existed, contracts, or grows, the end effect is always the same: It started off to a fresh (or possibly more recent) start 13.8 billion years ago. A broad variety of phenomena, including the large-scale structure, Hubble's law (i.e., the further distant galaxies are from Earth, the faster they travel away from us), and the cosmic microwave background (CMB), may be used to demonstrate this.

It nearly seems as if someone is thinking to themselves as they read this book, "Maybe life was brought to us by a space alien." However, how did they get it? Who or what is the space alien's creator?

I have a feeling that everyone with an I.Q. Anyone with an I.Q. who is above 65 and gives the aforementioned statement some serious thought is likely to come to the conclusion that any knowledge that resembles computer code and causes anything sophisticated to occur is the outcome of intelligence. However, if everything that exists is material stuff, then it would not have been possible. I'll say it again: without the development of the brain, intelligence would not have been conceivable.

Not all scientists are deaf to the truth. The fact that Click's finding constituted evidence of some type of directing intellect started to dawn on many experts. I can personally attest to this since I was able to read a book that made this claim more than 40 years ago. It disproved the idea that intellect, consciousness, or awareness were products of evolution and was published in 1975. The book's title was Intelligence Came First. A group of highly competent people who met once a month to discuss and read information wrote it. Ernest Lester Smith (1904–1992), a Fellow of the Royal Society, a distinguished scientific organization that supports scientific achievement, edited and published the book.

Intelligence Came originally generated a lot of debate when it was originally released. The book made the claim that DNA is computer code and pointed out that throughout evolution, requirements have existed independently of the organs that met them. Every new organ, according to the book's authors, was developed in answer to a particular necessity. What makes the brain unique, then? The participants and writers of the book came to the opinion that intelligence might first operate in its own environment. You'll find that researchers from the University of Virginia came to the same conclusion in a later chapter. They came to the same conclusion after 60 years of study on this subject: intellect and awareness don't need brains to exist.

Intelligence Came First is still in my possession. All except me have long since forgotten about it. It was yelled at by the Materialists in a vengeful tone. Consider the level of intellect needed to create any of these organs. They might all have developed accidentally (i.e., by natural selection then random mutations). It's probable that an eye, liver, or kidney's intricacy and complicated nature are the result of chance. However, it seems that in 1975, scientists held that opinion. Many people today still hold the belief or will not acknowledge they do not.

There is no question that intelligence—call it what you want; I prefer "Infinite Mind"—is responsible for the creation of all life. Everything began with DNA and tiny, single-celled creatures. The original life gradually developed into sophisticated beings with brains, kidneys, hearts, eyes, hearing, taste buds, and hearts. In the end, evolution culminated in the human. Was Infinite Intelligence pursuing a definite objective? Most probable, but we'll go through some potential outcomes. Whatever the situation, one thing is guaranteed. It may be more accurate to say that the Infinite Mind "pushes" rather than "encourages." It strives for harmony, expansion, and evolution. When a healthy body is at peace with itself, we say we are in harmony. But disorder is the polar opposite of harmony.

I was given the opportunity to host and create an Internet radio talk show called The Truth about Life in 2007 after reading the book many years earlier. I read and spoke with more than 100 truth-seeking writers during a three-year period. They included parapsychologists, medical professionals, metaphysicians, and quantum physicists. Near-death experiencers, theologians, psychiatric and psychological professionals, and other researchers interested in reality's veracity. I don't remember any of these cutting-edge individuals, with the exception of one speaker, having a materialist philosophy. He was unable to provide evidence to back up his assertions. Because it contradicted what science says, he could only assert that a certain assertion "cannot" be true. That was about as persuasive as a Christian zealot arguing, "It cannot be so because the Bible tells otherwise."

Darwin thought that mutations happened at random and that an organism's survival genes are handed down via generations. This makes reasonable, and it probably influences how creatures adjust to their surroundings as they change. How may this result in a kidney, an ear, or an eye?

Imagine, for example, that something moves in the appropriate way to develop a kidney as a consequence of a random occurrence. Or, to travel a bit farther back, to the development of the DNA code that allows life to exist. The natural direction of chaotic or spontaneous change is called entropy. It will halt any further advancement. Any progress gained will be undone by entropy, which is the inherent direction of spontaneous change toward disorder, before further progress can be created.

The argument based on chance is invalid for two reasons. First of all, there is a time constraint, and secondly, time is against the chemical synthesis of live things. Think of a bike lock with four dials. How probable is it that the four-digit code can be cracked? There are 10,000 different possible combinations (10x10x10x10x10). The chances of it occurring are low if the thief doesn't have enough time to attempt more than half (5,000) of the potential combinations. It's essential to take into account the ratio of possibilities to sequence complexity when determining if a random search is feasible for informative sequences.

This is the last word on the origins and development of life. The intricacy of the sequences, according to researchers who study this type of stuff, makes it impossible to look for the proteins that enable the development of life.

The reality of life and existence on the physical plane will be examined in the next chapter.

Behavioural Control

People tend to be overconfident. We are unable to compare our own abilities to those of others in fields in which we lack knowledge. You have undoubtedly heard of the Dunning-Kruger effect, a phenomenon that occurs often. It is astonishing how accurately this effect can be shown in almost every sociological exam. The result states that test subjects would often rate themselves above average when asked how skilled they are in an activity or how educated they are on a subject. The important thing to note in this situation is that they are not comparing themselves to others in the same hobby or academic subject, but rather to other people in general. The test subject is quite likely to claim that they are better than at least half of the other respondents to the survey if they lack a solid understanding of the skill of the remainder of the pool.

Effect of Dunning-Kruger

Despite how terrifying it may seem, this impact extends to those who have even had some expertise in a certain sector. The individual in this situation will never claim that they are worse than the norm. In a 2006 research, it was shown that 74% of the 300 professional fund managers polled felt they had outperformed the industry standard for job performance. 26% of the fund managers thought they were just average. This research demonstrates how the impact operates not just in practice but also across all industries, including investment. 100% of fund managers think they are above average, which is illogical as we all know.

It would be better to pick a fund manager from the 24% pool if one had to choose one from among the 300 poll participants. This group is less self-assured than the other group, but they are more likely to produce better yields. The amount of transactions an investor makes is positively connected with their confidence, while their yields are adversely correlated with the number of trades they make. Essentially, the more confident a trader you are, the more transactions you make, but ultimately, the less confident traders make fewer trades and profit more.

Ahead of the Pack

Following the conventional wisdom and thinking of the day has resulted in a number of bubbles, nearly always followed by a challenging fall. The first bubble I experienced occurred in 1999 with the emergence of tech 1.0 Internet enterprises. The stock prices of computer businesses like Yahoo, e-toys, and others were increasing at the time. As a result of the stocks' rapid ascent, it didn't take long before having an online presence and being publicly listed signified that your company was overpriced. This abruptly came to an end as traditional brick and mortar retailers caught up to their new internet rivals. I'll be the first to confess that I lost some money during this period, but I learned an important lesson from it: never put all your eggs in one basket.

The enormous overvaluations of several new tech businesses were the root cause of the early 2000s Internet bubble. These new IT businesses were mostly entering industries where physical shops had ceded dominance to online retailers. The value of software businesses skyrocketed as they were seen as rivals to these enormous department stores, but with a brand-new market that was ready to service more people than any physical shop could ever hope to. This concept spread so swiftly and widely that any digital firm that was in competition with a major brick and mortar business got assessments that they had no business receiving. Only a few individuals realized that brick and mortar businesses would only need to start selling their goods online in order to compete with these software startups; these big businesses already had the infrastructure and economies of scale necessary to crush any internet firm that stood in their way. The problem was that so many people were swarming to the sure thing that they missed out on the obvious signs that these companies could not survive. Most people weren't aware of this, and the common logic of the time was a great list of all the positives about the Internet, comments that still hold true.

Dependence is the mindset that encourages so many of us to just follow the crowd. You must base your search for investments on your own study and predictions of what could experience growth. The early 2000s IT startups attracted a lot of investors because of their reliance on third parties. The 1929 financial crisis and the 2008 financial crisis both have this similar issue as a contributing factor. People began doing what everyone else was doing since everyone was earning money; nevertheless, they should not rely on others' investment advice. Treasury bonds are a secure choice, therefore investing advice like that should be cherished. However, you shouldn't heed the advise to invest only in tech companies for the next two years since that's what the top twenty hedge fund managers do. Make sure, as a general rule, that you are completely aware of the investments you are making, their potential for development, as well as their risk for loss. The tech bubble would not have occurred in 1999 if more individuals had carried out this action.

I'm sure that there will be another bubble. Bubbles are cyclical and society as a whole cannot escape them, but if you look at the underlying worth of what is being regarded as valuable, you may see the bubble and potentially even short sale to profit. The 1637 tulip fever is one more illustration of this that I'd like to provide you. There will be another bubble because they always occur. Although there were bubbles before 1637, this one is generally known for being one of the most bizarre examples of herd reasoning.

The price of Dutch tulips peaked in 1637 after slowly increasing over the preceding six months. People all around the Netherlands were attempting to collect as many tulips as they could to sell to the foreigners who desired them as tulip prices soared at roughly 100 times their typical worth. Because the tulip's lost usefulness is so obvious, the tulip fall is intriguing. Due to the lack of a comparable flower in several regions of Europe, the tulip was simply becoming more valuable. However, its only use was as a cosmetic object. The novelty of the item would fade when enough people bought it, and with every flower that was seen in the rest of Europe, the tulips in the Netherlands lost value. It seems sense that the price would decrease the more often tulips were seen. Numerous investors lost everything during the sudden drop, since it only took the tulip's worth four months to return to where it had been almost a year before. The takeaway is that every bubble has some element of reality, just as there was in the tulip bubble. People did, in fact, realize that tulips were appreciating in value, but they vastly underestimated it. The worth of such businesses is obvious when contrasted to the businesses that failed, even if several IT firms went on to be the best performers of the previous fifteen years. Your investment decisions must always be made by you, and only after you have established the fundamental worth of the asset you are purchasing.

The Fallacy of the Gambler

A gambler enters one quarter after another into a slot machine while seated. Is he coming any closer to hitting the jackpot with each quarter? Of course not, but the gambler is confident that if he plays the machine for a little bit longer, he will win the jackpot and be able to leave the casino with the money. The concern that if he leaves, someone else may seat at his machine and grab his earnings is one of the things that keeps the gambler there. Even the most logical individuals may fall victim to this reasoning, which is present in the investment industry and is simple to see from the outside.

You start to be concerned that your new favorite stock is about to go downhill after three days in a row when you finished ahead. Let's consider the grounds on why you hold this assertion. You may have seen that equities often show gains for no more than three days before reporting losses, or you may have knowledge of the underlying business that makes you think the stock will decline. When an investor withdraws money too soon, it almost often happens due to pattern recognition or a misleading indicator rather than any fresh information regarding the organization. The investor who withdraws their money early is committing the gambler's fallacy by comparing the closing stock price of tomorrow to that of yesterday, even if the two are unrelated. The closing price over the previous several days is not a reliable sign of any trend in either a good or negative direction. The stock price tomorrow will depend on a variety of variables. To disprove the guffaw's fallacy In this case, you need to consider your reasons for selling the particular investment. If patterns hold the key, you should reevaluate the likelihood that the stock will in fact fall or rise. There is more reliable information available, and the seemingly trending non-sequential random closing prices will just skew your opinion in the wrong direction.

The gambler's fallacy might cause an investor to hang onto a stock for far longer than they should and sell it too soon. There is no logical reason why a stock should suddenly turn around after multiple days of poor closings, yet two bits of information keep the trader locked in and making losses. One reason is because they are following a pattern that suggests that stocks cannot continue to decline if the industry is generally healthy, but this has no influence on the specific closing levels. Despite the fact that the two pieces of information are contradictory, the investor's mind is still drawing a conclusion. Second, the investor is concerned about further financial loss. If losing money is precisely what they are frightened of, it may seem unusual that they would retain their money in a losing stock, but selling the stock is a way of acknowledging you are losing.

The gambler's fallacy is when an investor concentrates on the money they have already lost rather than the money they would save by selling a stock. These two numbers have absolutely nothing in common, as in the other cases. The investor is in a pickle by trying to combine these two contradictory pieces of information. The gambler's fallacy may be extremely difficult to see in oneself, but the best approach to prevent it is to constantly consider the underlying asset and treat each investment you make as if it were entirely independent of any prior investments you may have made. The transactions you make today are unaffected by the deals you made yesterday.

Is Investing In Non-Fungible Tokens Worthwhile?

NFTs seem to provide a unique, high-risk opportunity to generate significant gains, but be warned that this only sometimes occurs. They are appealing to risk-taking investors. Consider investing in an index fund rather than a Pop-Tart cat GIF if you're searching for a more reliable way to put your money to work, even if it is less flinchy and has the same cultural cache.

You must first establish a digital wallet if you want to take a risk and join the world of non-fungible tokens. This is where you will store your cryptocurrency and NFTs. You must then search for NFTs on websites like OpenSea.io or Rarible, choose one you like, buy the appropriate cryptocurrency for that specific NFT, and make your purchase.

It's then a waiting game. Your NFT's value depends on how much someone else is willing to pay for it, so both you and your Pop-Tart cat are at the whim of the market.

The Benefits of Investing in Non-Fungible Tokens (NFT)

Non-fungible tokens (NFT) are a special kind of tokens that cannot be exchanged because of their unique distinguishing characteristics. Simply said, non-fungible tokens have distinctive qualities that prevent replacement or exchange.

They are ERC-720 compliant and have mostly been used in the storing of crypto-collectibles like artworks;

offering a means of proving authenticity and ownership; and in crypto gaming. Non-fungible tokens are tokenized representations of real-world or digital assets.

NFTs gained momentum in 2017 with the release of the cryptocurrency game known as CryptoKitties. The game Cryptokitties, which was a pioneer of NFTs, allowed users to collect, save genetic materials, breed, and sell virtual cats. Amazing, yes?

The Ethereum network had a spike in CryptoKitties transactions in December of the same year, totaling more than 12,000 transactions, which led to an increase in the cost of breeding kittens.

Why Should I Invest in Non-Fungible Securities?

NFTs have shown to be a profitable kind of investment for some of the reasons listed below:

Value is Created for the Taken Asset: NFTs provide a medium via which physical objects, such as works of art, may be taken, preventing duplication of such works and reserving ownership for the creator. This in turn generates interest in the art work and, thus, value for it.

It offers investors more liquidity: Taking an equity position gives investors greater control over their equity when they need it. When a virtual landowner decides to rent out his or her virtual space to advertisers or influencers for a fee, while still maintaining ownership over the property, that is an example. In this instance, a portion of the virtual land still belongs to the owner but is liquidated as rent.

Potential for development and growth: NFTs have potential for the growth and development of the land sector. For example, in real estate, tying NFTs to land parcels has shown to have significant potential for growth and development. Owning and owning virtual property gives you the freedom to do anything you want with it. You might choose to rent it out or set up a safe and secure business for advertising or online sales.

Creating Sense Non-fungible tokens (NFTs), a tool that allows anyone to monetise digital content, may seem to be a passing fad, but with over $10 billion expected to be traded in the third quarter of 2021 alone, it is clear that this emerging technology is developing into a significant industry. Musician 3LAU collaborated with cryptocurrency firm Origin Protocol in March of this year to create a specialized platform to sell his new album as an NFT, which it ultimately sold for $11.6 million. Famous visual artist Beeple famously sold a tokenized digital artwork for $69 million through Christie's auction house, and the NBA's Top Shot, which allows fans to buy and sell tokenized video clips of basketball game highlights and is owned by cryptocurrency platform Dropper Labs, has generated over $715 million in transaction volume.

In response to this enormous expansion, both individual artists and companies from a wide range of industries, including entertainment, retail, music, consumer goods, fashion, and more, have been actively exploring ways to interact with the world of NFTs. While some sellers have chosen to create their own NFT market places, the majority have discovered that a partnership with a third-party platform is more practical because it can lower startup costs, provide access to a larger customer base, and provide beneficial supplemental services like marketing, legal, and technological support.

What is an NFT market place?

In contrast to platforms like Spotify and Netflix, which offer limitless access to digital content in exchange for a monthly fee, NFT platforms are designed on the premise that, like physical content, digital content can be scarce, limited in quantity, and can, therefore, be meaningfully owned and traded. These platforms use blockchain technology to verify the provenance of digital content, similar to how a traditional auction house might confirm that a given work of art is in fact the original and not a replica. Some platforms even give users the option to "burn" items, which further emphasizes the idea of scarcity for these digital goods. Additionally, blockchain-based transaction logs may facilitate ownership attribution by automatically sharing a portion of revenue from second-hand sales with the original creator each time the NFT is sold.

Of course, as with any investment in a new capability, choosing the wrong marketing platform can seriously backfire. When it comes to leveraging a rapidly-evolving new technology like NFTs, the best option isn't always obvious. It's crucial to understand the landscape of platforms now available and choose which will be the greatest match for your NFT offerings in order to avoid making expensive mistakes.

What kinds of markets are there?

While there are many factors to take into account, we've found that categorizing NFT markets on a spectrum from enhanced to streamlined may be very helpful. Broadly defined markets enable a wider variety of NFTs and give more constrained, general services to sellers, while enhanced markets are highly specialized and provide a more complete service experience.

Streamlined platforms include systems like OpenSea and Rarible that support both auctions and fixed-price sales for a wide range of NFTs and more closely resemble conventional platforms like eBay, Ety, or Mercars. These marketplaces primarily focus on facilitating efficient transactions, often providing payment infrastructure to take both credit cards and cash. as well as cryptocurrency payments in Bitcoin, Ethereum, and sometimes other speciality tokens. Because of their breadth and the minimum additional services they provide, these platforms often have sizably large and diverse user populations.

On the other hand, enhanced market places tend to concentrate on more specific niches and provide a variety of value-added services including minting (creating the NFT itself), marketing, curation, price suggestions, portfolio trackers, and even fully-fledged games built on top of the NFTs. For instance, the NBA's Top Shop focuses solely on basketball collectibles that the platform packages and markets, while SuperRare focuses on visual art and offers extensive curation and recommendation services.

Finally, SORARE, which focuses on digital sports cards, hosts fantasy soccer competitions that include the cards users purchase on the platform.

These specialty services may provide a lot of value, but they are unavoidably expensive. Augmented platforms often have a higher "take rate," or transaction fee, as well as higher upfront setup costs to account for the resources needed to build up, integrate, and maintain a variety of specialized tools and experiences. Streamlined markets often have cheaper startup and ongoing costs, but they could still need sellers to use their own resources or hire outside experts to develop, mint, and advertise their NFTs.

Where Can I Invest In Assets?

"Whether you work or not, assets put money in your pocket, and liabilities take money out of your pocket."

Robert Kiyosaki, author

Stocks

Moderate Risk

Having stock entails having ownership rights to a corporation. On stock exchanges, shares of stock are exchanged via stockbrokers. The Amsterdam Stock market (AEX), which originally opened its doors in 1602, was the first stock market. Since that time, more than 60 stock exchanges have sprung up worldwide.

Any risk profile is accessible for stock shares: low/medium/high:

Blue chip stocks are low risk investments. These are shares in reputable businesses that provide items to a dependable consumer base. Utilities are one example of a high-yield, low-risk investment industry.

Companies that are well-established but not doing well at the moment or businesses with issues that have a lot of promise might be considered medium risk stocks. Telecommunications is a medium-risk industry since there is a clear market demand for the goods that are now offered, but there is also a probability that a single technical breakthrough might completely alter the market.

Stocks in industries like biotech, where technical advancements may instantly make or destroy corporate fortunes, are considered high risk. Also exceedingly dangerous are small-cap stocks. Small capitalization, or "small cap," refers to a company's whole market value. Smaller businesses have a lot of room for expansion. However, they also have a high risk of bankruptcy!

Bonds Minimal risk

The three key concepts of bonds are as follows:

Bonds aren't stocks, either.

Bond values often increase when the value of equities declines. (Therefore, a portfolio with a medium level of risk should be diversified and include both stocks and bonds.)

Bond values fall when interest rates rise. Also the opposite.

With a bond, you, the investor, enters into a borrowing arrangement with the bond issuer for a certain amount of time. Bonds are categorized as a fixed income instrument and are often issued by both companies and sovereign governments. This implies that while you possess the bond, the bond's issuer will continue to pay you interest. The 'coupon rate' for each bond determines these interest rates, which are referred to as 'coupon payments'. The 'maturity date' of a bond is the last day on which it may be sold. The bond's issuer will reimburse you for your initial investment when the bond reaches its maturity date.

The issuer's credit rating is a significant factor in determining a bond's value. For instance, the issuer of a US Treasury bond has a superb credit rating. There is a slim danger that the US government may break its commitment to you and refuse to return your money when your bond matures.

However, the issuer of junk bonds has a poor credit rating. There are two effects of this. First off, there is a greater danger that the issuer may fail, rendering your bond worthless. Second, since junk bonds are riskier, they will have significantly higher "coupon rates"; in other words, you will get a larger return from the bond.

Bonds come in a variety of forms, such as callable, convertible, and zero-coupon bonds. Investing in a bond fund is a secure method to get exposure to bonds without having to understand all of their nuances.

Funds

Low danger

Mutual funds enable you, the novice investor, to spread your risk over a variety of assets at once and gain from the expertise of experienced investors.

For the sake of fund members who later enjoy the rewards (or losses), a fund manager will invest in a range of assets. Active and passive funds are two categories of funds. Active funds often demand higher fees since they are managed by actual people. Since passive funds are not managed, their costs are often cheaper.

Funds are often managed in accordance with a certain product, industry, or risk profile.

Indices Funds

A market index is tracked by index funds. This indicates that the fund represents the worth of a complete market at once rather than focusing on a few specific assets. For novice investors, this is a fantastic strategy to diversify risk.

Exchange-Traded Funds (ETFs)

Passive funds make up 98% of ETFs. Because they are less expensive than managed funds while yet providing the same advantage of distributing investor risk, their popularity has exploded. Between 2003 and 2020, there were 276 fewer ETFs globally than there were in 2003—over 7,600.

ETFs may function similarly to index funds and follow a certain index. The SPDR S&P 500 Trust ETF, which follows the US S&P 500 index of the top 500 US firms, is a well-known tracker ETF. One of the primary benchmarks for the US equities market is this tracker fund. Since its creation in 1993, it has represented firms with a combined value of $374 billion and generated returns of 10% on average annually. ETFs often don't pay dividends, but this one did in 2020; the dividend yield was 1.78%.

ETFs are also offered in certain industries and assets (stocks, commodities, currencies, bonds, cryptocurrencies) outside from tracker funds. Like funds, ETFs are sometimes focused on certain risk profiles.

ETFs are much less expensive than index funds in terms of expenses. The 'expense ratio' of a fund or ETF is what you need to pay attention to. An example of an expense ratio is the 0.095% offered by the SPDR S&P 500 ETF. Accordingly, for every $1000 invested, the fund will cost the investor $0.95. On the other hand, cost ratios for index funds typically range between 0.5% and 0.75%.

There will often be a transaction charge of $10–$20 if you wish to exchange your ETF share.

Commodities

moderate risk

In the actual world, commodities include tangible goods like food, precious metals, and oil. Commodity exposure is possible via CFD trading or investment in commodity funds.

The most well-known commodity is gold. Consider always include some gold in your portfolio. Gold is seen as a refuge of safety. Its cost generally increases very slowly. Additionally, gold prices often increase when stock markets decline.

Property Investment's Benefits And Drawbacks

We covered how you may make a sizable income from different real estate investment strategies in the last chapter. Everyone enjoys money and wants to be able to have that additional income to assist with the times when their house doesn't have as much money coming in.

Others who work in real estate do so out of a desire to help others fulfill their goal of owning a piece of land.

Whatever your motivation for wanting to start investing in real estate, you should be aware of some of the major benefits and risks associated with doing so. And that is what this chapter will focus on.

Benefits:

Leverage may be used to lower your monetary outlay: When you have the capacity to leverage, even if you just pay cash for around 20% of an item, you will be able to "possess" the whole thing. This separates investment in rental property from other kinds of investments.

Consider that you own a $100 rental unit. The twenty bucks needed to buy it, however, are beyond your means. Therefore, you will be required to pay the whole sum of $100. You have access to the leverage option to lower your out-of-pocket costs. As a consequence, for people with little extra money, rental properties are great first investments. When you decide to sell, the power of leverage and the free equity you have amassed will work together to provide a fantastic cash-on-cash return on investment. Leverage has helped a lot of individuals who have invested in real estate to become affluent.

The biggest benefit of real estate investment is the opportunity to acquire free equity. The mortgage and any other costs associated with the properties you own are paid each month in rent by the tenants who occupy them.

As a consequence, as time passes, your home equity will increase and your mortgage debt will drop.

You will be able to take advantage of the equity that has built up when you decide to sell the home.

It is comparable, for instance, to making monthly contributions to a housing investment account but receiving no interest.

Your tax burden will be reduced since you'll be allowed to deduct different types of rental property from your income. This happens even if you didn't pay the financed expenditures out of your own pocket.

If you own the property through what is known as a "one-person real estate LLC," all deductions may be reported on your regular tax return. A bigger tax refund will be the outcome.

In essence, you may spend your income on the property and then pay taxes on it. Simply put, you will have more money that is just yours if your taxes are reduced.

Eventually, you'll be able to provide a monthly cash flow: To be able to make money when you decide to sell the properties in 10 years or more is the ultimate goal of investing in real estate. However, having a monthly cash flow that goes into a reserve account is the greatest way to guarantee that this happens.

This will be useful in the event that your renter quits abruptly or if a natural disaster necessitates the restoration of the property.

Your cash flow will be limited at first since you are just beginning off, just as it is with everything else. But don't give up; your cash flow will become better every year. This will happen because you may raise the rent, so raising the rental property's revenue, while simultaneously increasing your monthly mortgage payment and keeping tabs on your property's expenses.

You should be able to make a little profit of around $100 per month after a few years. You may decide whether to keep all the proceeds for yourself or to invest them in your rental property to speed up the process of paying off your mortgage, depending on the state of your property.

Whatever you chose, having the choice of what you want to accomplish will be beneficial. Please remember that you shouldn't anticipate having this choice when you first begin.

One of the perks of real estate investment that does not provide instant fulfillment is the joy of providing someone a house. Whatever happens, you'll be pleased with this.

By donating a home to someone who would not otherwise be able to live in one, you will be giving back to someone in a manner that is not monetary.

Additionally, if you take good care of your renters, they will return the favor by making sure that they do all possible to pay the rent on time.

Tenants need to be seen as clients, not as a source of income. You are helping to ease one of their worries by giving them a place to live since, like you, they are people with their own issues to worry about.

Risks

Investment loss is the danger that real estate investment has that is by far the most significant. the worst case scenario for a failed investment.

You shouldn't let this stop you from making real estate investments. You will encounter other risks when it comes to investing, but this is only one of them.

The only thing you stand to lose if you invest in flipping homes is your income since there is a possibility that you may be wounded while working on the modifications to the property.

The truth is that many individuals who start investing in real estate flipping have little to no insurance, and when they get harmed, they have to spend money on fixing whatever they've damaged or hurt rather than investing it in the home.

Not only do they not have adequate insurance for themselves, but also for their property.

The market is one of the risks that you will be unable to manage. The market will have ups and downs, which is a sad fact. Additionally, there will be mishaps, firms will close or relocate, and the local real estate market will suffer along with the health of the economy.

Customers changing their thoughts and ultimately pulling out of the sale at the last minute is the biggest cause that will hurt your investment.

You'll have to cope with the effects of each one of them. However, the things that will happen have nothing to do with you and are out of your hands. All you can do is take the blows as they come and hope you can recover to continue.

Due to the high expense of repairs, you can end up with a house that was not worth the money spent on it. Furthermore, it may not even be fixable.

It is obvious that the repairs will be costly and will lower the earnings you may have been able to make if it didn't demand so much effort.

Unfortunately, this has the drawback that you are obligated to either disclose the property's shortcomings to any prospective purchasers or fix the issues before selling the home.

If you don't have the money to buy the home you want and make the required repairs to it, you run another risk of being in trouble.

Real estate investment requires significant financial resources since you must pay certain upfront costs before you start to get a monthly income. (Later in this book, we'll talk about your real estate investment budget.)

However, you will need to plan your spending with the few funds you do have so that you can not only take care of the real estate property's needs but also your own survival.

Various Forms Of Financial Investment

Stocks

When you invest money in a stock, you officially join the partnership as one of the owners. Stocks deal with possession shares, also known as value shares. Whether you profit or lose money on a stock depends on a number of factors, including the success or failure of the company, the kind of stock you possess, general market conditions, and other factors.

Regularly include stocks and stock common assets in your venture portfolio may be quite beneficial.

In order to make a bigger profit down the road, you must first research the market and choose the finest company to invest in.

ASSESSING STOCKS IN THE MARKET: Stock Evaluation

The questions to ask when you choose between the stocks you're considering are similar to the questions you'd ask if you were buying the whole company since when you buy a stock, you're buying a portion of the company.

What products does the company offer?

Is it accurate to say that they are well-liked and excellent?

Is the company doing well overall?

How has the group behaved in the past?

Our competent, seasoned directors in charge?

Are our labor expenses reasonable or unreasonably high?

Does the organization have significant obligations?

What obstacles and challenges does the company face?

Does the stock warrant its present price?

You need a system for evaluating the value of multiple stocks since each company is a different size and has made a different number of bids. A common and efficient way to accomplish this is to look at the stock's earnings. All publicly traded companies must submit quarterly unaudited 10-Q filings and annual 10-K filings to the Securities and Exchange Commission (SEC) in order to disclose their financial results.

You can discover the company's current earnings per share, or EPS, in those reports, its annual report, or on its website, assuming you really look at those things. The organization's total earnings is divided by the quantity of offers to arrive at that ratio. The results of firms of varying sizes might then be examined using this per share figure. EPS is one indicator of a company's current strength.

The cost-to-income ratio, often known as the P/E ratio and the most frequently used indicator of stock value, may be calculated by dividing the current price of a company by its earnings per share. P/E essentially tells you how many donors are contributing for every dollar of an organization's revenue. For instance, if Company A has a P/E of 25 and Company B has a P/E of 20, investors would pay more for each dollar that Company A acquires than for each dollar that Company B acquires.

Although there is no perfect P/E, there is a market normal at some arbitrary point. Over the long run, that number has generally been 15, but it has fluctuated between higher and lower numbers. While development financial backers often buy businesses with higher than average P/E ratios, esteem financial backers typically go for firms with somewhat low P/E ratios—below the flow normal.

While P/E may be a useful indicator, it shouldn't be your primary criterion for evaluating a company. For instance, there are instances when you should carefully consider a company with a P/E that is greater than average for its industry if you have reason to be optimistic about its potential in the future. However, keep in mind that if a stock has an unexpectedly high P/E, the company will need to generate much larger income in the future to justify the price. On the other end of the spectrum, a low P/E may be a sign that a company is really having financial difficulties or that a significant increase in value is possible. One of the decisions you must make before making a purchase is this.

A P/E ratio must be almost as useful as the revenue figures it is based on. Even if there are guidelines for describing revenue and financial reports from an organization are assessed, there may still be inconsistencies in profit reporting. You've probably seen articles in the financial news about companies that consistently make money. This occurs when an organization has to provide reports for earlier periods due to an accounting error or other discrepancy. Incorrect or inconsistent income justifications might weaken P/E as a measure of stock value.

Although P/E is the most often mentioned ratio of stock value, it is not the only one. Additionally, you'll hear stock gurus discussing metrics like ROA (return on assets), ROE (return on equity), etc. These acronyms may at first seem confusing, but as you learn to know them, you may discover that they help with answering some of your questions about an organization, such as how productive it is and how much responsibility it is carrying.

Competent stock exploration is one way to explore particular stocks in more detail. The company where you have your record may provide research that comes from both internal and external sources. Additionally, independent research conducted by investigators not affiliated with a corporate organization is available, as are consensus studies that compile the findings of many investigators. A section of this investigation is free, but a another investigation has a price tag.

There have previously been unresolvable issues at companies that provide public organizations with speculative banking administrations since specialists sometimes felt under pressure to do thorough reviews of such equities. However, in order to agree to rules meant to restrict any such anticipated irreconcilable events, corporate organizations must establish strict divides between their venture banking and stock investigation departments.

INVESTMENT DEFINITION FOR BONDS

A bond is a financial commitment made by a financial backer to a business, government, bureaucratic agency, or other entity in exchange for interest payments over a defined duration as well as payment of the principal at the bond's creation date. Treasury securities, office securities, business securities, city securities, and that's just the tip of the iceberg, are among the diverse range of securities available. The many types of security common assets are similar.

When you invest money in securities and other financial assets, you run the risk of losing money on your investment, especially if you bought a single bond and need to sell it before it matures. Additionally, security shared asset expenses fluctuate in a similar manner. The risk will also vary depending on the kind of bond you hold.

Learning The Investment Rules

The stock market is simply one form of investment you may make when you look at the investing world. More investigation reveals that almost everything may be an investment. If it is set up properly, even your best friend's emu farm may be a wise investment.

We won't be concentrating on your best friend's emu farm just now. We'll talk about wise investments you can make to begin began on the path to financial independence and freedom. Understanding how these investments will enable you to become wealthy without taking huge risks is the main goal of this chapter. Additionally, you'll discover that starting even with a few dollars is pretty simple.

One of the most pervasive myths about investing is that "it takes money to make money." The false notion that you must make a substantial investment in order to get significant profits permeates this way of thinking. While something is accurate mathematically, it may not be accurate practically. You know, starting off doesn't need a large amount of investment funds. As we've already said, all you need to get started is something.

So let's look at the several categories of financial assets you might include in your total investing portfolio.

Understanding Financial Assets

There are several assets available for investment. Some are rather simple, while others are really intricate. In an effort to make everything as simple to understand as possible, we will examine each one.

Stocks

The most popular financial asset that can be traded is stocks, often known as equities. Stocks are only a portion of ownership in a publicly listed business. Businesses are traded "publicly" because anybody may invest in them.

You can't simply walk out and purchase shares, of course. On a stock market, such as the one on Wall Street in New York City, the stock of these corporations is exchanged. To achieve this, you must engage the services of a stockbroker to carry out the transaction on your behalf. Because of this, brokers deduct a portion of your winnings. They must generate their compensation as well as some income for the organization they work for. There is nothing wrong with it, but you should be aware that not all brokers are the same. Knowing their prices will prevent you from being taken advantage of.

Buying cheap and selling high is the key to stock trading success. The truth is to purchase as cheaply as you can and sell as expensively as you can. It becomes a little tough at this point. Brokers and investors often succumb to their own greed. They thus often bet excessively. They take on too much danger when this occurs. As a result, they can wind up making risky transactions that might cause them to lose a lot of money.

The fact that equities generate dividends is yet another intriguing feature. A shareholder's portion of the profit is paid out as "dividends" at the conclusion of the fiscal year. Ordinarily, dividends amount to cents per share. However, you may earn a sizable sum of money if you own a number of thousand shares. Investors choose "blue chip" businesses because of this. A company is referred to be "blue chip" if their reputation and proven track record make them stalwarts in their sector. These are businesses that consistently make a profit. As a result, investors rush to buy as many of these companies as they can.

You may use a broker to purchase and sell shares on your behalf if you want to trade equities. However, you require a significant quantity of investing cash to execute this. The "rich" investors club steps in at this point. Rich investors may combine their funds in these clubs so that experienced brokers may do the legwork on their behalf. They are often referred to as "hedge funds." This is a snazzy name for groupings of affluent investors, which might include both people and big businesses.

Mutual funds, index funds, exchange traded funds (ETFs), and investment accounts like a 401(k) are all ways for retail investors, or individuals without a lot of money to invest, to get a piece of the action. Retail investors' funds are combined in these accounts, and the earnings are subsequently distributed to all participants. These accounts often give returns that are in line with the market. This suggests that you should anticipate an annual interest rate of between 4% and 6%. After your investment has expired, you have the option of withdrawing it or rolling it over. The majority of investors take some of their money out and roll the remainder over.

Retail investors are pooled together in financial vehicles known as mutual funds. These funds provide a wide variety of equities. This indicates that these funds don't invest in just one kind of business or sector. The fund may include a group of businesses from diverse sectors. Taking this action is intended to lower risk. Money managers, in a sense, strive to steer clear of relying too much on the success of a particular business or sector.

Another kind of financial tool designed to profit from a diverse selection of equities is an index fund. An index fund is linked to one of the main stock indexes, such as the Dow Jones Industrial Average, the S&P 500, or the NASDAQ, which distinguishes it from mutual funds and stocks. You have the option of investing in the index fund that best meets your needs, depending on your own preferences. Due to the Dow Jones' inclusion of the 30 biggest American corporations, it is often considered to be the largest of the main indexes. The S&P 500 also offers exposure to the 500 biggest American firms. These two indexes don't concentrate on any one industry. They concentrate on a variety of companies, if anything. As a result, you may invest in a fund that matches your specific interests.

Regarding the NASDAQ, this index primarily tracks technology businesses. Therefore, if you are eager to invest in the technology industry, this would be your top pick. There are, of course, other sorts of index funds that follow a variety of particular industries, including mining, gas, oil, and industrial enterprises. Finding out which sectors give the highest returns depending on your expectations is the best approach to decide the sort of industry you want to invest in. For instance, the need for heating during the winter months tends to boost revenues for the mining, oil, and gas industries. Similar to how consumer demand for fuel increases in the summer, oil corporations often see higher income during this time.

You must do these kinds of evaluations in order to choose where to invest your money. By keeping up with the news on major news sources like Bloomberg, MSNBC, CNN, Financial Times, or Market Watch, you may do this pretty simply. Of course, there are a ton of other sources of business news. But you should constantly cross-reference what you read.

You may also invest by buying shares via a process known as "private equity." Typically, this kind of investing entails getting shares directly from the business. The regular investor has access to this option via large firms, but it may be challenging to get a foot in the door. Consequently, a lot of affluent people finance startups. In return for money, these investors purchase a portion of a new firm. These funds are used by the firm's founders to develop their operations and the company as a whole. The owners of private equity may benefit if the company succeeds. Just consider the investors who purchased shares in Facebook and Google at the beginning. It may be unlikely for you to invest in a startup with the potential of Google or Facebook, but if you can buy into a business that is acquired by a major corporation, you stand to gain significantly.

Commodities

Some investors choose to invest in commodities over equities, which they would rather do. Commodities are tangible items that may be delivered to the location of your choosing. Oil, gas, metals (both industrial and precious), agricultural goods, livestock, and manufactured goods are some of the most popular commodities traded on financial markets. These products are purchased and sold on financial markets using futures, spot, and exchange-traded funds (ETFs), three types of investment vehicles.

When you hear the word "spot," it denotes contracts that are valid for the delivery of the underlying asset at the current rate on the market. This is important to remember since market circumstances have an impact on current market pricing. Investors will thus rush to get any available oil contracts if there is news of a probable oil shortage. The cost increases as a result. Therefore, contract holders stand to gain greatly.

Investors employ "futures" contracts to lock in pricing so they won't lose money on the open market. A futures contract bargains for the delivery of the product at today's pricing in the future. Producers benefit since they can guarantee the sale of their output, and investors may rest easy knowing that prices won't suddenly change without warning. Depending on the investor's expectations, these contracts may be purchased or sold.

Investors may pool their funds using ETFs as a mechanism. Following that, these funds are invested precisely in a certain commodity. Therefore, you may invest in an oil ETF if you're interested in getting exposure to the oil market. The ETF offers rewards depending on how well oil is doing. Therefore, you benefit if the price of oil increases and investors profit. Your investment would be lost if oil prices fell. That is the risk that comes with ETFs.

It should be highlighted that ETFs are favored by investors as a means of investing in commodities that they believe have a promising future without having to deal directly with the commodities themselves. After all, the majority of investors aren't very interested in receiving oil barrels at their residences.

Including valuable commodities like gold

Occasionally, you may hear about investing in gold and other precious metals, such as silver, platinum, and palladium. Despite having investment appeal, gold is a commodity that is exchanged. This is due to the fact that investors often withdraw funds from the stock market and invest them in precious metals when the market volatility subsides. You have two options for getting exposure to gold: either purchase actual gold or get "paper" gold. ETFs that are based on gold are referred to as "paper gold." The majority of investors choose this option because they want to be exposed to precious metals without taking the chance of getting gold bars delivered to their home.

You may always invest in silver if you think gold is too pricey. Silver is a considerably more affordable choice. The price of platinum and palladium is typically half that of gold. So, if you're eager to have exposure to precious metals, you may think about investing in an ETF.

FOREX

The FOREX market is subject to a wealth of information. Given that you are dealing only with currencies on this market, it is the most liquid market on the earth. This implies that you exchange US dollars for euros. Naturally, you could apply this to any currency in the world. There are two methods to invest in this market. One is a FOREX ETF in which you may invest your money and delegate the grunt work to money managers. The second option is for you to directly trade FOREX. You may get your hands dirty in the FOREX market with the help of tools like MetaTrader 4. You may cut out the middlemen, similar to day trading (where you trade stocks directly), to make financial choices on your own.

You do need to get acquainted with the market's characteristics in order to invest in FOREX. However, since FOREX is a 24-hour market, you will discover that it is a terrific method to invest in your spare time if you are interested in doing this yourself. You might trade at night or on the weekends as a result. Additionally, you might save a lot of money on fees and commissions. It is definitely a fantastic choice for anybody who wishes to get practical experience.

Cryptocurrency

Cryptocurrency investing has to be seen as a contact sport. Cryptocurrencies are not for the faint of heart since they lack the steadiness of investments like equities or commodities. For instance, investors in Bitcoin experienced a rollercoaster of emotions. initially off, when it initially began, one Bitcoin could be purchased for as low as $2. After then, it shot up to a peak of $20,000 per coin before plummeting to roughly $5,000. It has now recovered to roughly $10,000. What a crazy journey. Some investors made out well along the road and became millionaires. Others were utterly destroyed. Cryptos are not for the weak of heart because of this.

However, you can still participate in this market by either investing in a crypto ETF or directly investing in cryptocurrencies by buying them yourself and reselling them (just as you would gold). Crypto-based ETFs are a relatively new kind of investing tool. As a result, before investing in one, conduct your research. But there are reliable ETFs that provide investors access to a variety of currencies, including Bitcoin, Ethereum, Litecoin, and many more. If you don't have $10,000 to buy a single Bitcoin, the beautiful thing about ETFs is that you can acquire a portion of ownership of one. Your financial situation improves as Bitcoin's value rises. The value of your share decreases if the valuation decreases. Nevertheless, it's worthwhile to check into because cryptocurrencies seem to be the future. Who knows if you invest in a cheap currency that can soar in value as Bitcoin did?

Bonds

Another well-liked kind of investing is bonds. Bonds are a kind of debt that is issued by companies or governments. Then, when governments and businesses utilize them to raise money, they are negotiated among investors.

There are sovereign bonds first. These are issued by governments and may either be bought directly via an auction or sold on a stock market. A set of investors admitted to the bond auction, for instance, receives bonds directly from the US Treasury. The Federal Reserve (FED) is the principal purchaser of these bonds. After then, the FED releases dollars into circulation. These dollars are supported by the Treasury's issued bonds. As a result, a standard dollar note is backed by debt, namely debt that the US Treasury has generated.

Corporate bonds, on the other hand, are backed by the company issuing them. The sale of assets or the complete liquidation of the firm would thus be used to cover the bankruptcy of the corporation if it were to become unable to pay off these obligations at some time. The existing bonds and other obligations would then be paid in full with the revenues.

It should be mentioned that compared to corporate bonds, sovereign bonds are less hazardous. But not all countries are as stable as others. As a result, it poses a bigger danger for their bonds to fail.

Bonds are a viable investment option, particularly if you're seeking for long-term holdings. You have two options for getting them: via public auctions or through your broker. Bonds were formerly used to pass on wealth from one generation to the next. However, keep in mind that due to inflation, a $100 bond had a higher value thirty years ago than it does now.

However, you could obtain high returns on a bond if you have money that you don't intend to spend right away.

Using Etfs To Combine Passive And Active Investing

ETFs have been discussed extensively thus far. ETFs have grown in popularity because they provide investors the freedom to put their money precisely where they want to. Because of this, investors have no influence over mutual funds. Investors only entrust a fund manager with their funds, and that is the end of it. This is not a negative thing, as we've already said. The ETFs, however, provide you a greater chance to do so if you like to be more hands-on.

We will thus examine how you may use ETFs to be both an active and a passive investor in this section.

passive investment

For passive investors, ETFs are excellent. Compared to the typical mutual fund or investing account, they provide larger returns. All you are doing when you invest in an ETF is placing your money into a sector, company, or commodity that you believe has the potential to generate substantial returns. ETFs often pay out more since there is more risk involved. However, you can reasonably be certain that you will see a profit.

Now, depending on the ETF's characteristics, you won't need to move a muscle. You only get a statement detailing the status of your account at the end of each month. That is rather unactive. Your broker may sometimes contact you and ask you to add money to your account or even roll over your contract. Your broker could sometimes attempt to upsell you to an ETF that performs better. That's ultimately up to you.

You can get strong short-term returns from ETFs, particularly if the fund performs well. Even if they won't make you wealthy over night, you may anticipate steady returns, especially in sectors and with products that have a proven track record.

investing in action

You may now buy ETFs on your own as part of day trading if you're a more hands-on trader. Additionally, you have the option of managing your account in-person with a broker. This is often only available to wealthy people who satisfy the requirements to work one-on-one with an account manager. You may phone your broker and ask them to liquidate your investment and shift you into something else if you fulfill these requirements. After all, you are paying for this.

Similar to this, if you're eligible for a wealthy investors club, you may withdraw your funds whenever you choose. You may request that your money manager give you a check for your capital plus returns, unless the contract requires you to wait a particular amount of time. In this kind of arrangement, you engage the account manager to do the grunt work while you monitor your investment's return and choose the kind of investments that are made on your behalf. This would be a fantastic choice for you if you prefer to jump right into the action.

Principles of Financial Management

All successful investors work to develop a discipline that will help them make informed investment choices; this discipline is based on the idea that you must have a distinct investing philosophy. This is why using a loose-lipped technique often results in outcomes that are at best subpar.

Additionally, having the proper mentality is essential to being a successful investor. In order to assist you steer your investing philosophy and ensure that you get the highest returns, we're going to look at three golden laws of money management.

Don't risk more than you can afford to lose by investing.

This rule is as unbreakable as they come. You often hear of stock market participants taking out a mortgage on their house. Then, in addition to still paying on the home, they lose a significant portion of their investment when the market crashes. It goes without saying that this is a poor decision.

So, before making an investment, consider how much you may conceivably lose without seriously harming your finances. That's what it is if it's just $500. Never stake your family's future on the stock market.

There is no way to predict what will occur at any particular moment since risk is a necessary component of investment.

Always have a strategy.

You should always have a strategy, even if you want to be a passive investor. Based on the kind of investments you have made, your broker may help you visualize the sorts of returns you can anticipate. If you are a more practical person, you may sit down and estimate how much money you could anticipate to earn. Then, consider that while deciding whether to roll over all of your earnings or possibly to set aside a portion for other uses, including debt repayment. In the end, having a strategy will always be advantageous, even during difficult times.

Give your funds the opportunity to increase

All investors want to get significant profits right immediately. However, you may not immediately see astronomical returns. Give your money a chance to increase because of this. Your investment money will gather pace as it continues to increase. You'll eventually be able to generate large profits. Because of this, having patience is a quality that all investors should possess. If you are not ready to commit the time necessary for your money to develop, you may want to think about more risky investment strategies, such establishing your own company.

You'll be set for life if you follow these golden guidelines. In reality, you'll discover that when you know what to do and where you are heading, generating money via investing is really fairly simple.

Mistakes New Investors Should Avoid

The errors that rookie investors commit are the antithesis of the golden principles. So let's examine the top five mistakes that novice investors make.

not broadening

In essence, you are placing all of your eggs in this one basket. Without diversification, you inevitably wind yourself pinning your hopes on a single stock, sector, or asset class. In the worst-case scenario, you get completely destroyed. Even in the best-case scenario, the results are disappointing.

Investigating the numerous instruments is the remedy for this error. A mix of mutual funds, ETFs, commodities, and even private equity is a strategy used by successful investors. This will provide many income sources while helping you to mitigate losses.

assuming excessive risk

Even while risk is a necessary component of investment, taking on too much of it may be detrimental. Investing in something you don't understand is maybe the greatest risk you can take. You are taking on too much risk, for example, if you are asked to invest in a firm where you are unsure of how it will earn money. Because of this, when they cannot understand how an investment would generate a profit, investors pull back. This is something that you must always have in mind.

Using excessively little investment capital

Because diversity reduces risk, beginning investors try to invest in as many different things as they can. However, not everyone should make investments. You must choose which assets are suitable for you. The most crucial thing is to understand what each sort of investment entails before making a move. In order to avoid making mistakes, it is preferable to start with one sort of investment before going on to another. Before moving on, it's usually a good idea to become proficient at one.

being persuaded to invest

Salespeople are taught to win over clients without truly discussing the details of investment. It's better to hit the brakes if an aggressive broker or sales executive is tailgating you. Every time you feel pressed to make an investment, a desperate marketer is probably trying to convince you to do so. Always invest in instruments you are familiar with, and learn as much as you can. You may do your own research to be proactive in this way. The next time you get a call, you will know who is calling and from where.

FOMO, or the fear of missing out

This psychological phenomena is real. The best illustration of this is Bitcoin. Investors experienced FOMO as the value of Bitcoin soared. They piled on in an effort to catch the wave. Some were successful; others were devastated. You've already missed the opportunity if you see that everyone is racing to make an investment. Let the excitement fizzle out. When everything has calmed down, you may enter and get some serious discounts.

Investments

What are investments, exactly? In essence, they are things that you put money in with the hope that it will grow for you. Investments are different from bets because, unlike bets, you are expected to know precisely what you are investing in and how it will make you money.

But when we ask "what are investments," we want to know "in what form do they exist?" As a consequence, knowing what you are going to purchase and sell on the stock market, as well as how you plan to interact with it, is essential for every investor.

The Stock Market and Stocks

The stock market is where you may purchase, sell, and trade different investments, as was mentioned a few chapters back. As a consequence, there are many ways to make money in this place.

But what really is the market's main product? Stocks are one means of doing this. As was previously said, stocks serve as proof that you have invested money in a firm in return for ownership of its assets and income.

Stocks are great investment vehicles since a company's success as a whole has a direct impact on its profitability. A company's worth improves when it performs successfully. The value of your shares also rises as the company's worth increases.

By selling your stock ownership to another party at the current market price, you may profit from your investments. By trading under the right conditions, you may, for example, effectively gain more than 200 percent of your original investment if you bought inexpensive stocks and the market value of that company rose by multiple digits.

You can still make money off of your stock ownership, however, if you decide to do so. A business may choose to give its shareholders a percentage of its earnings. As a consequence, you must carefully examine the tiny print on the stocks to see what advantages you may have as a shareholder before deciding to invest in a firm.

The point being made is that equities are often a good option for novice investors. Many wealthy investors, like Warren Buffet, gained their money exclusively by investing in equities before retiring. Of course, the corporation determines the stock's likelihood of success.

Therefore, it is crucial to understand how to monitor and project where a company's performance is going. For instance, you may sell your shares before the price lowers if you think the firm is in jeopardy. In this manner, a significant portion of your wealth will remain intact when you quit the business.

The Different Stocks

We typically presume that all stocks have the same appearance when we think about them. However, in practice, stocks are frequently offered in two formats. These are what they are:

Common

Almost often, when people talk about stocks in general, they are talking about this kind. Common stocks are just what their name suggests: common. They represent your claim to a share of the firm and its dividends and are traded publicly on stock exchanges. Simply said, this is the category into which the majority of equities on the stock market fall.

As a result of their rising capital, stocks have the benefit of offering significant returns over time. In other words, a company's stock price increases when it does well. Whether the stocks have yet to be sold or are still held by an investor, it doesn't matter. All stocks will increase in value as long as the business is profitable.

Naturally, the opposite is also true. If a firm performs badly or is about to file for bankruptcy, its stock loses all of its value. No matter how much you originally paid for such stocks, you won't make any money from them.

Preferred

The benefits of preferred stock are the same as those of ordinary stock in that you have a stake in the firm and a claim to its dividends. It is more constrained, however, since you don't have the same voting rights as with ordinary stocks. In other words, preferred stock won't provide you the ability to have a vote in how the company is operated.

However, it does provide a set dividend. Preferred shareholder distributions will be consistent throughout, in contrast to ordinary stocks, where the dividend value may change based on the company's performance. The dividend is often far more than what a common stock would provide.

Another benefit is that you will always get payment before ordinary investors if the firm is liquidated. But remember that your obligations to your creditors must come before your own.

Preferred stocks may finally be termed. The company may purchase your shares at a premium if it needs to recover possession of its equities for whatever reason.

At first glance, preferred stocks seem to behave more like bonds than genuine shares. It is positioned in the center. Simply stated, preferred stocks are different since they provide more dividend sharing and the potential to be paid off first when the company shuts.

Rights to vote and stock classes

Can a firm establish a new stock class for its shares? Yes, kind of. Even though stocks are either common or preferred, companies have created techniques to change their shares to create new classes. Why would businesses act in such a manner? In either scenario, wouldn't they sell a portion of their company to total strangers?

The fact is that ownership has little impact on businesses. The right to vote is more significant. The preferred stock has shown that control over a company's management is more significant than ownership.

As a consequence, businesses are coming up with innovative methods for raising money from investors while maintaining the voting rights of a limited, sometimes concealed number of shareholders. Because of this, the different classes are typically linked to the different levels of voting power available.

For instance, company XYZ may distribute a large number of shares, each of which entitled the holder to 10 votes. Only one vote may be cast using the remaining shares. As a result, one group will get 500 votes, while the other will only have 50, assuming there are 100 shareholders split evenly between the two groups. Keep in mind that a company's majority is determined by the total number of votes cast, not by the number of shareholders.

How do stock options work?

In essence, options are a different kind of stock with a more nimble pricing mechanism. Buying an option is almost like gambling since the price of the underlying stock may change depending on how the firm performs over the course of the option term.

That seems like a hazardous plan, don't you think? Not at all, no. You have more buying power over those equities for a brief period of time when you acquire an option rather than a standard individual stock. This means that you have a limited window of time to acquire or sell that stock. Even better, you can sell or trade an option without really being the owner of it.

Of sure, the continual price fluctuation might be harmful. It is possible that prices may drop significantly for a number of times. This suggests that you could sustain losses over time, depending on the company's performance.

So if you want to invest in a high-risk, high-reward method, stock options are perfect. But because of it, they are hazardous for anyone who are inexperienced with them. Learn the fundamentals of the other stocks and assets before thinking about adding options to your investing portfolio.

The Additional Investment Types

In order to purchase and sell stocks and other assets on the stock market, there is no need that you physically own the securities. In reality, the documents verifying your ownership of these assets will be what you deal with constantly here.

As there is no possibility of the actual item being destroyed or damaged during each transaction, this offers a reasonably safe environment for doing commerce. Depending on the stock, some items could not even move from where they are now put. Only one person may legally transfer ownership of them.

Additionally, the stock's kind directly affects risk. Of course, risk and reward are inversely correlated. Regardless of the status of the economy, certain companies are always wise investments, while others have the highest potential profits but also carry a higher risk. To balance the risks and rewards, a savvy investor would know which stocks to purchase.

It is now important to educate yourself on the various stock kinds available for purchase.

Money and commodities

Cash and commodities are the lowest risk investments. They are considered as the core of any stock market since the volume of trades in these stocks directly affects the health of the economy. These stocks are often viable investment options that may act as a crucial safety net for your portfolio even if the economy worsens.

This kind of commodity's poor return is its principal drawback. The investor's profit margin is relatively low since they pose the least risk.

Gold

One of the oldest stock options still on the market today may be this metal. Gold has been traded for a variety of goods even before the Egyptians constructed their pyramids. Gold is attractive, making it a secure initial investment. But keep in mind that a lot of this allure comes from scarcity and anxiety. As a consequence, owing to factors outside your control, the price of gold changes.

If you want to invest in gold, bear in mind that the only thing protecting you from a price decline is something outside of your control. In actuality, gold's price varies greatly. This commodity's single saving grace is the fact that the price of gold has never been lower than zero.

To make the most of gold, one must also understand the concept of scarcity. In essence, when there is a severe scarcity and fear, gold prices rise. As a consequence, gold could be a good investment for you if you wish to safeguard your money in case anything disastrous occurs.

Deposits in cash and other financial products

Banks provide these investments, as the name suggests. The most popular forms of bank products are savings and money market accounts. A cash deposit, on the other hand, is only a loan to the bank in return for the money being paid back to you with interest.

Gold and other bank assets are regarded as low-risk investments. In practice, you may only get yearly returns of 2% or less on these kinds of investments. You would comprehend that 2 percent would not be enough to earn money on these investments if you understood how inflation works.

In essence, these are secure options, but if you want to increase your money dramatically over time, there are better options available.

Cryptocurrencies

Cryptocurrencies are a more recent kind of investment since they are uncontrolled digital investment options that are often provided outside of the stock market. You may have heard of one of these currencies, Bitcoin, which has seen significant growth in recent years.

However, since they are so new and contain so many unknowns, you should stay away from these alternate forms of investment. Due to the rise in the amount of scams utilizing digital currencies, several countries are contemplating regulating them. Therefore, it will take a long time for Bitcoin and similar technologies to become widely accepted in the market.

Therefore, cryptocurrencies should be avoided for the time being as long as stock exchanges do not recognize these investment options.

Bonds and Investments

These are yet another low-risk investment option offered by organizations like the government and your typical commercial company.

corporate and governmental bonds

Although bonds are not issued by banks, they are comparable to cash deposits. You are essentially loan that institution your money when you buy a bond from the government or a private company in the hopes that they will return it to you with interest at a later time.

The only time you won't receive your money back from bonds is if the individual who issued them fails for any reason, which is very unlikely. With government savings bonds, it is unlikely to occur.

Corporate bonds are riskier due to the higher possibility of a private firm failing. A bond does not provide you ownership of the company's assets or earnings, as contrast to stock or shares.

What you must understand is that over a number of years, both corporate and government bonds may provide returns of up to 3% on your investment. This suggests that you run the risk of losing purchasing power if you take money out of the bond. After all, an annual growth rate of 3% falls short of the inflation rate.

Securities based on mortgages

A loan and a security are comparable. However, there are certain real estate mortgages attached to this loan.

The possibility of profit is what sets securities apart from bonds. Mortgage-backed securities have the ability to pay interest to investors on a monthly basis, unlike bonds, which only do so when the period has passed.

On the other side, what makes these securities intimidating is their complexity. There are too many factors to take into account when figuring up your monthly payment. The dangers also tend to be larger based on the mortgage's conditions.

As a result, investors should only think about this investment choice if they have a lot of prior market expertise. You should start with the lower-risk, more straightforward investing alternatives as a novice.

Funds for investments

In essence, an investment fund is a pool of money from several investors that is used to buy a range of items, including but not limited to stocks, bonds, and other tradable assets. The finest indicator of a market's success, funds are great since they track the market index.

Investment funds

In a sense, this investment option is a proxy investment. It will be managed by an agency who you have given permission to invest your money and find methods to make money off of it.

Mutual funds are secure because of the speedy diversification provided by their distinctive architecture. You gain from them either when you sell your money if market values increase or when they generate interest.

The only drawback to this option is that maintaining them will cost you more money. In practice, a portion of your cash would be utilized to cover the cost of your manager's services as well as any agents they would employ to maintain your investments.

Consider this investment to be a mid-tier option as a consequence. Start off with less risky assets to get some practice managing your own funds. Once you are confident in your skills, you may quickly diversify your portfolio utilizing mutual funds.

Index Funds

This fund will enable you to quickly diversify your money, much like mutual funds do. The only thing separating them is the passive management of index funds. This suggests you'll spend less money overall, enabling you to retain more of the returns on your investment.

On the other hand, the quantity of your returns will be precisely proportionate to the market index. Your returns will decrease if the index does, and vice versa.

This investment option can be ideal for you if you want to invest money in something and then completely forget about it.

Traded-Deposit Funds

ETFs function similarly to traditional funds. Since it is one of the few funds bought directly from the stock market, it stands apart. As a consequence, it gives you even more control over how much you spend on them, and as a result, you will pay less in maintenance costs.

However, the profitability of the fund is inexorably correlated with the success of the market index. You can get around some of these limitations by making an investment in an index fund like the S&P 500.

As a consequence, new investors should consider investing in this fund.

Options for Retirement and Other Savings

Bank and other financial institution accounts are an option for these investments. The risk and return for retirement options may vary since the objectives and length of each product vary. If you are a beginner, think about these options as soon as you can, but go cautiously and perform extensive study before opting to invest in them.

Furthermore, several investment alternatives are known for having lengthy maturity periods. Only if you are dedicated to patient, long-term planning should you include them in your financial strategy.

Finally, they are not only chances for investments. Alternatively, you may use your retirement plans as a tool to diversify your financial portfolio. The only need is that you have access to the money invested in these plans, thus they must have reached maturity in order to be fully exploited.

401K

A retirement plan offered by a business that is required by the US government is called a 401K. The prospect that your employer may match, or at least partly match, your prior contribution may encourage you to consider such an investment option.

For investors who want to be safeguarded, a 401K's matching element is what makes it so alluring. In contrast, 401Ks function in a way that is comparable to a conventional mutual fund in terms of diversification. It means that a management is in charge of the money, and you are required to pay them regularly for their services.

401K accounts may only be opened by those who are actively working. The only person who can provide you such a chance is your present employer. As a consequence, you have a limited number of 401K options over your lifetime.

IRA

IRAs are either tax-free or have their earnings tax-deferred. It suggests that a portion of your money won't be used to fill government coffers.

Additionally, you have more investment options with an IRA than a 401K. The money may also be used to purchase other items like mutual funds, investments, and stocks.

In conclusion, if you want to reduce your risks, have more control over your money, and swiftly diversify your portfolio, an IRA is a terrific option. The secret to success in this situation is to quickly max out your plan.

Annuities

An annuity is more of a financial agreement between you and a firm, usually an insurance provider. In this scenario, you pay an insurance provider up front with the intention of receiving recurring reimbursements. It is comparable to a salary if you are already retired in that you get it on a regular basis.

The benefit of annuities is that there is no risk involved. The main problem is that they lack a financial motivation. It is a great method to get a steady income if you are retired, but there is little room for growth.

They are not anyone's greatest option for investments because of this.

Additionally, it shouldn't serve as a launchpad for other investing concepts.

Actual Estate

Real estate is one of the most profitable financial options accessible, whether you are buying, refurbishing, or selling homes. However, the significant return in real estate comes with a lengthy list of risks and costs. Real estate is a high-risk investment, despite the fact that there are specialized strategies for reducing your risks in this field.

Until they have understood the principles of other investing opportunities, novice investors should stay away from this option. Furthermore, your work here requires a substantial cash commitment.

Property

Currently, it is difficult to locate a building, whether for commercial or residential use, for less than $50,000.00 for the complete structure, without repairs. As a result, it could seem as if people with little to no money are precluded from making this investment. Crowdfunding, however, has shown to be an effective alternative source of financing for investors in this field. The only drawback is that you will have to divide the earnings with others according to the guidelines you established. With this investment method, it might be challenging to find the proper safety buffer. The safety margin is simply the difference between your asking price based on the property's current fair market value and your original expenses of buying and flipping the property.

Consumers won't be eager to buy the house if the margin is too high. A margin that is too small will result in a loss of money. You may sell your house for a sizable profit if you can find the sweet spot between costs and pricing.

Real estate investing involves more than just buying cheap and selling high. Additionally, you have the option of renting out the houses to customers, providing steady income from your long-term investments.

Securities Trusts

Due to the fact that it pools the money from various investors and invests it in a number of businesses that generate income, this sort of investment functions similarly to a mutual fund. Investment Trusts are the most affordable option for property-based investments since they can be bought, sold, and exchanged on the stock market.

An investment trust is one of the safest property-based investments for beginners since you are not needed to buy, remodel, or sell real estate. If you were selling real estate, you would generate more revenue. However, you will consistently get income over time.

What to Invest in NOT

Only a portion of the investments that are accessible to you on the stock market and elsewhere are represented by those that are mentioned above. While not recommended, cryptocurrencies and annuities may be profitable provided you know what you're doing or, at the very least, have a sizeable safety net in case things don't work out.

You should steer clear of a lot of financial opportunities at the moment. Either they are poor investments or the present economic climate is to blame for their poor performance. Here are a few investments that beginners should never think of doing.

Low-Quality Mortgages

A subprime mortgage is a dirty bar at the extreme end of a red-light district if investing options are buildings. These mortgages are intended for borrowers who are the least trustworthy and are most likely to default on a loan. By purchasing one, you may be confident that the money you just lent to someone else will never come back to you.

Dollar Stocks

Companies often sell their shares for no less than $5.00, which is seen as a poor price. But other businesses trade for less, and Wall Street calls these equities "penny stocks." The typical starting price is $1.00 or 50 cents, which might be alluring to novice investors. Due of their limited numbers, even little changes in their pricing might produce substantial changes in your income.

But it's their cunning that makes them lethal. A penny stock often signals a company's impending bankruptcy. It's one technique for dishonest businesses to sell off all of their shares and walk away from the stock market with a sizable sum of cash.

They serve as fronts for many pump and dump schemes that leave investors with worthless shares.

Crap Bonds

Because a large return on investment typically includes a significant amount of risk, they are known as high-yield bonds. Investors may find junk bonds enticing, especially in a market with low interest rates.

Like penny stocks, a junk bond is often a sign that a business is failing or is about to go bankrupt. The term "junk bond" refers to a corporate bond in which you almost certainly will lose money if you hold it.

By purchasing a bond via a mutual fund, you may lessen the risks, but this does not provide a permanent solution. Avoid buying any bond from the firm out of caution if you don't know enough about it or aren't sure how to predict its performance.

Individual Placements

A private placement is a stock that has not been placed on a stock exchange. Private placements are immediately off-putting since you have to wait to invest until you are an authorized investor. Moreover, how does one get accredited? Either you make $100,000.00 a year or you have a net worth of at least $1,000,000.00.

Private placements are troublesome in and of itself, but what makes them so is that they are usually used by dishonest marketers who make you promise a lot of benefits without warning you about the risks. In other words, you'll be gambling by investing in something about which you don't fully understand it.

Dual Digit Return

Certain stock prices seem too good to be true. If you hear of an investment that is marketed to you as having more than

10% yearly returns, you should exercise caution. The usual gibberish like "it is insured!" and "it is backed by the government!" is then said, followed by the all-too-common "it is the next (insert famous firm here)!"

It is wise to remember that no investment plan can guarantee a profit. No stock ever offers double-digit returns, despite the fact that some are insured and others are supported by the government. Actually, even the best businesses seldom provide returns of 10%. While some just provide the customary 2-3%, others are kind enough to pay 5%. There you have it.

Just keep in mind that anything that appears too wonderful to be true certainly is.

To Sum Up

So which investment plan should you start with? Everything depends on you. However, a solid foundation is required if you want to keep a strong position in this sector.

To achieve this, start with equities and progressively add other investment alternatives to diversify your portfolio. It is a great strategy for getting a sense of the market without going over budget. If things doesn't work out, you may simply back out.

In other words, start with stocks and then go on to other assets.

www.ingramcontent.com/pod-product-compliance
Lightning Source LLC
Chambersburg PA
CBHW050239120526
44590CB00016B/2157